GREEK MYTHS

Children's Treasuries

GREEK MYTHS

Illustrated by Milo Winter and Others

Sandy Creek
NEW YORK

Sandy Creek
NEW YORK

An Imprint of Sterling Publishing
387 Park Avenue South
New York, NY 10016

The stories in this volume have been adapted from
Favorite Greek Myths by Lilian Stoughton Hyde and
A Book of Myths and Legends by Jean Lang.

ISBN 978-1-4351-4586-3

Distributed in Canada by Sterling Publishing
c/o Canadian Manda Group, 165 Dufferin Street
Toronto, Ontario, Canada M6K 3H6

Printed and bound in China
Lot #:
2 4 6 8 10 9 7 5 3 1
07/13

CONTENTS

IN THE GOLDEN AGE, EVERYONE WAS GOOD AND HAPPY.

IT WAS ALWAYS SPRING.

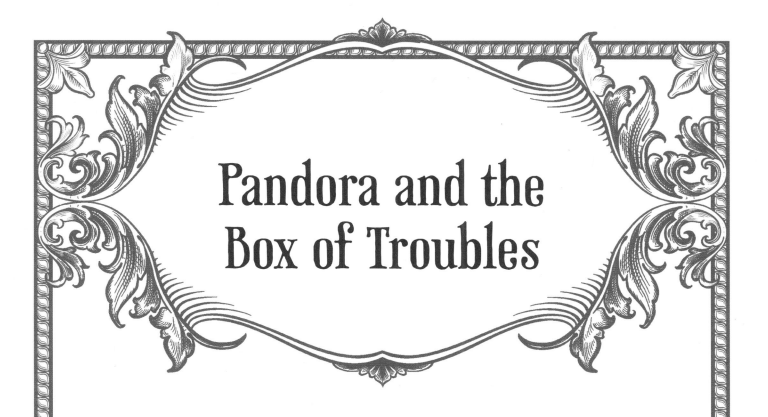

Pandora and the Box of Troubles

A very long time ago, in the Golden Age, everyone was good and happy. It was always spring; the earth was covered with flowers, and only gentle winds blew to set the flowers dancing.

In those wonderful days there lived two brothers, Prometheus and Epimetheus, who were members of a race of giants known as the Titans. The Titans were enemies of the gods, and Prometheus, especially, had angered the gods when he stole fire from their home on Mount Olympus and gave it to man, that men might use it to fashion tools to better their lives. The gods had punished Prometheus severely for his theft. Even though they later forgave him, Prometheus knew to beware of the gods.

One day, Prometheus left to go on a long journey, and before he went, he warned Epimetheus not to receive any gifts from the gods.

After Prometheus had been gone for some time, Mercury, who was the messenger of the gods, came to the cottage of Epimetheus, leading by the hand a beautiful young woman whose name was Pandora. She had a wreath of partly opened rosebuds on her head, delicate gold chains twisted lightly around her neck, and a filmy veil which fell nearly to the hem of her tunic. Mercury presented her to Epimetheus, saying the gods had sent this gift so that he would not be lonesome.

Pandora had such a lovely face that Epimetheus could not help believing the gods had sent her to him in good faith. So he paid no heed to the warning of Prometheus, but took Pandora into his cottage.

Soon, the gods sent Epimetheus another gift. This was a heavy box, which was brought to the cottage with directions that it was not to be opened. Epimetheus let

Out rushed a great swarm of little winged creatures, and before
Pandora knew what had happened, she was stung all over.

the box stand in a corner of his cottage; for by this time he had begun to think that the caution of Prometheus about receiving gifts from the gods was altogether unnecessary.

Often, Epimetheus was away all day, hunting, or fishing, or gathering grapes from the wild vines that grew along the river banks. On such days, Pandora had nothing to do but wonder what was in the mysterious box. One day her curiosity was so great that she lifted the lid a very little way and peeped in. The result was similar to what would have happened had she lifted the top off a beehive. Out rushed a great swarm of little winged creatures, and before Pandora knew what had happened, she was stung all over. She dropped the lid and ran out of the cottage, screaming. Epimetheus, who was just coming in at the door, was stung, too.

The little winged creatures that Pandora had let out of the box were Troubles—the first that had ever been seen in the world. They flew about and spread themselves everywhere, pinching and stinging whenever they got the chance.

THIS LITTLE HOPE PERSUADED PANDORA TO LET HER OUT.

After this, people began to have all manner of illnesses; and instead of being always kind and pleasant to one another, they became unfriendly and quarrelsome. They began to grow old, too. Oh, it was a sad thing for the world, when all those wicked little Troubles were let loose!

All the Troubles escaped from the box, but when Pandora let the lid fall so hastily, she shut in one little winged creature, a kind of good fairy whose name was Hope. This little Hope persuaded Pandora to let her out. As soon as she was free, she flew about in the world, undoing all the evil that the Troubles had done, as fast as one good fairy could undo the evil work of a swarm of Troubles. No matter what evil thing had happened to poor mortals, she always found some way to comfort them. She fanned aching heads with her gossamer wings; she brought back the color to pale cheeks; and, best of all, she whispered to those who were growing old that they should one day be young again.

So this is the way that Troubles came into the world, but we must not forget that Hope came with them.

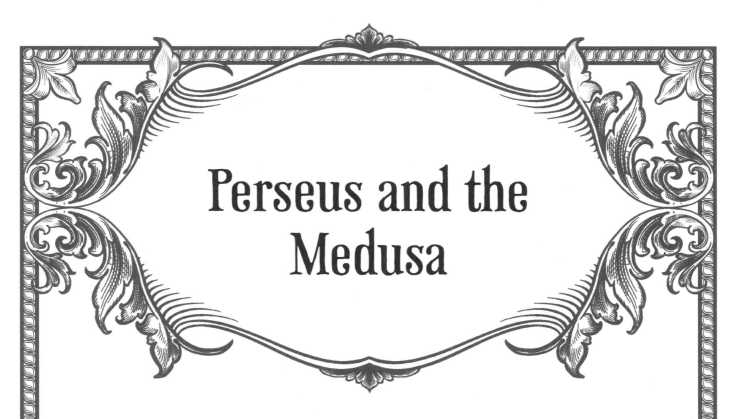

Perseus and the Medusa

Acrisius, the king of Argos, was once very much frightened by a prophecy of the oracle of Apollo that he would be killed by his own grandson. Acrisius had only one child, a daughter named Danaë, and to prevent the oracle's prediction from coming true, he had Danaë shut up in a strong, brass tower. Nevertheless, when the spring came, the news reached the king that a golden child, with blue eyes and clear white skin, had been born in the tower. King Acrisius was quite beside himself with fright when he heard this news. He immediately commanded that Danaë and her golden child should be put into a brass-bound chest and allowed to float out to sea.

So Danaë and her baby, whom she named Perseus, were put out to sea, where the chest drifted all night. In the early morning, the tides brought it close to the island of Seriphus, where it became entangled in a fisherman's nets. The fisherman, whose name was Dictys, took Danaë and her baby to his brother Polydectes, who was the king of that island. King Polydectes was willing that Danaë should stay on the island, and Danaë found a good home there; for Dictys and his wife took her into their own cottage, and did all they could to make her comfortable.

Perseus grew up a strong, handsome youth who attracted much attention from the people everywhere. This made King Polydectes extremely jealous. The stronger and handsomer that Perseus grew, and the more admiration his youthful strength and beauty called forth, the more King Polydectes hated him. He finally thought of a plan for getting rid of Perseus forever.

It so happened that, on a rocky, dreary, barren island which lay in the midst of the sea, a long way from the island of Seriphus and from every inhabited country,

THE FISHERMAN, WHOSE NAME WAS DICTYS, TOOK DANAË AND HER BABY
TO HIS BROTHER POLYDECTES.

there lived three fierce sisters who were called the Gorgons. These strange sisters had faces like women, but they were not like women in any other respect. They had eagles' wings with glittering golden feathers, scales and claws of brass and iron, and great fierce-looking tusks. Worst of all, instead of hair, their heads were covered with venomous snakes, that were always twisting themselves about, and putting out their forked tongues, ready to bite anything that came within reach. The youngest, who was called the Medusa, had a face so terrible that anyone who looked at it was immediately changed into stone.

Now King Polydectes knew all about the Gorgons, and he made up his mind that there could be no better way of getting rid of Perseus than to send him after the Medusa's head. So one day he called the young man to him, and told him that he was soon to marry the Princess Hippodamia, and wished Perseus to bring him the head of the Medusa as a wedding gift. He added that, unless Perseus brought the head with him, he must never come back to the island of Seriphus again. And he shut Danaë up in an underground dungeon, and said she should not come out till Perseus did as he was ordered.

Perseus did not know where the Island of the Gorgons was, nor how to find it. Staring out to the western sea, where he thought it was, he suddenly noticed two people standing on the sands by his side. One was a very tall woman who wore a helmet on her head and carried a very bright shield on her arm and a lance in her hand. The other was a young man with wings on his cap and sandals, a winged staff in his hand, and a crooked sword that shone like a flame at his side. Perseus knew that the tall woman was Minerva and the young man Mercury, and that they had come to help him. This was just what he had been expecting, for the gods of Olympus often appeared at just the right time, ready to help those who were brave and determined to do all they could for themselves.

First Minerva told Perseus how to find the Island of the Gorgons. She said that he must ask the Three Gray Women, who were cousins of the Gorgons, since nobody else in the whole world could give him the necessary information. Next, she said that when he had found the Gorgons, he must not touch either of the older ones, because they were immortal, and that he must by no means look at the Medusa, lest he be turned into stone. Then she took from her arm her own bright shield, which reflected in its surface anything held near it, and told Perseus that when he was ready to strike off the Medusa's head, he must look at that terrible face only in this shield, which she would lend to him for that purpose.

Now it was Mercury's turn. He lent Perseus his own sword, which was so sharp that it would cut through brass or iron. This was the only sword that would cut through the Gorgon's scales. Then he offered to show Perseus the way to the home of the Three Gray Women, who lived in Twilight Land, somewhere among the mists that rose from the sea.

They journeyed far to the north, until they came to a land of cold, fogs, and darkness. At last, in the dim light, they could faintly see three very old women coming toward them. They had long gray hair and long gray garments; even their faces were gray; and they groped along in the fog as though they could not see. They seemed to be quarrelling about something. As they came nearer, the quarrel proved to be about the use of their one eye; for they were so very old that they had only one eye and one tooth among the three.

"Be quick, Perseus! Now is your time," said Mercury. "Seize their one eye, and then you can force them to tell you how to find the Gorgons. They will never tell you of their own free will."

So Perseus seized the eye, and would not give it back till the Gray Women had answered his questions. They said that the only way to find the Island of the Gorgons was to ask the Hesperides, the daughters of Night.

So Mercury and Perseus traveled far to the west, over land and sea, to the Garden of the Hesperides. The nymphs of the Garden received Mercury and Perseus in a friendly manner. They said they had been expecting the hero who was to slay the Medusa, and should be glad to help him. They pointed out to Perseus the Island of the Gorgons, already dimly visible on the horizon. Then they brought him a pair of winged sandals which had

So Perseus seized the eye, and would not give it back till the Gray Women had answered his questions.

the power to bear their wearer through the air as fast as Mercury's own; the helmet of darkness, which belonged to Pluto, and made its wearer invisible; and the magic pouch, in which he could safely carry the head of the Medusa. Perseus was now well armed, and ready for his work. With Minerva's bright shield, Mercury's sword, the winged shoes, the helmet of darkness, and the magic pouch, he had not so very much to fear after all from the terrible Gorgons, and he was eager to begin the battle.

Thinking that the Gorgons would be asleep by midnight, he waited until that time, and then flew straight to the Island. As he hovered over it, like a great golden hawk, he looked into Minerva's shield, by the light of the full moon, and saw a frightful sight. There were all three of the Gorgons fast asleep. Around them was what looked at first like a confusion of strange brown rocks, but the seeming rocks were really men and animals that had been changed to stone by the sight of the Medusa's face.

Keeping his eyes on the shield, Perseus dropped lightly down, and in a flash he had cut off the Medusa's head and dropped it into the magic pouch. Then he sped away on the winged sandals, and it was well that he had these sandals and Pluto's helmet to make him invisible; for the remaining Gorgons woke and sprang after him with a terrible cry. He could hear the rushing of their gold-feathered wings, the rattle of their brass claws, and the hissing of the snakes on their heads. But these sounds and even their terrible cry soon died away; for the Gorgons could not follow far a foe that they could not see. So Perseus got safe away with the Medusa's head.

When the news that Perseus had returned with the head of the Medusa was spread abroad, what a rejoicing there was in the island of Seriphus! King Polydectes alone was not glad. Nevertheless, he pretended to be, and he made a great feast, at which the minstrels sang of the great deeds of Danaë's son. As all the enemies of his mother and himself were gathered together at the feast, Perseus held up the head of the Medusa before them, and so made an end of them, King Polydectes and all.

In a flash he had cut off the Medusa's head.

King Midas and the Golden Touch

Once upon a time, there lived a very rich king whose name was Midas. King Midas was fonder of gold than of anything else in the world. When Midas was a very little child, he used to watch the ants running back and forth over the sand near his father's palace. It seemed to him that the ant-hill was like another palace, and that the ants were working very hard, carrying in treasure, for they came running to the ant-hill from all directions, carrying little white bundles. Midas made up his mind, then, that when he grew up, he would work very hard and gather treasure together. Now an aging king whose great wealth could not be measured, Midas

King Midas was fonder of gold than of anything else in the world.

could scarcely bear to see or touch any object that was not gold. He made it his custom to pass a large portion of every day in a dark and dreary apartment, underground, in the basement of his palace. It was in this chamber that Midas kept his wealth.

Here, after carefully locking the door, he would take a bag of gold coins, or a gold cup as big as a washbowl, or a heavy golden bar, or a pouch of gold dust, and bring them from the dark corners of the room into the one bright and narrow sunbeam that shone through the dungeon-like window. He valued the sunbeam for no other reason but that his treasure would not shine without its help. And then would he reckon over the coins in the bag; toss up the bar, and catch it as it came down; sift the gold-dust through his fingers; look at the funny image of his own face, as reflected in the burnished circumference of the cup; and whisper to himself, "O Midas, rich King Midas, what a happy man art thou!"

Midas called himself a happy man, but felt that he was not yet quite so happy as he might be. He would never feel completely fulfilled unless the whole world were to become his treasure-room, and be filled with yellow metal which should be all his own.

Midas was enjoying himself in his treasure-room one day, as usual, when a shadow fell over his heaps of gold. Looking suddenly up, what should he behold but the figure of a stranger, standing in the bright and narrow sunbeam! It was a young man, with a cheerful and ruddy face.

As Midas knew that he had carefully turned the key in the lock, and that no man of mortal strength could possibly break into his treasure-room, he concluded, of course, that his visitor must be more than mortal, perhaps even someone sent by the gods.

"You are a wealthy man, friend Midas!" he observed. "I doubt whether any other four walls, on earth, contain so much gold as you have piled up in this room."

"I have done pretty well—pretty well," answered Midas, in a discontented tone. "But, after all, it is but a trifle, when you consider that it has taken me my whole life to get it together. If one could live a thousand years, he might have time to grow rich!"

LOOKING SUDDENLY UP, WHAT SHOULD HE BEHOLD BUT THE FIGURE OF A
STRANGER, STANDING IN THE BRIGHT AND NARROW SUNBEAM!

"What!" exclaimed the stranger. "Then you are not satisfied?"

Midas shook his head.

"And pray what would satisfy you?" asked the stranger. "Merely for the curiosity of the thing, I should be glad to know."

Raising his head, he looked the lustrous stranger in the face.

"It is only this," replied Midas. "I am weary of collecting my treasures with so much trouble, and beholding such small piles after I have done my best. I wish everything that I touch to be changed to gold!"

The stranger looked at Midas, and smiled a mysterious smile.

"Done," he said.

King Midas did not quite believe the stranger had the power to grant his wish. Nevertheless, he rushed from his gold-filled basement to a nearby grove and, standing under an oak tree, raised his hand to touch one of its branches. Immediately, the branch turned into the richest gold, with all the little acorns as perfect as ever.

Midas laughed triumphantly at that. Then he touched a small stone which lay on the ground. This became a solid gold nugget. Then he picked an apple from a tree, and held a beautiful, bright gold apple in his hand.

O, there was no doubt about it. King Midas really had the Golden Touch! He thought it too good to be true. After this he touched the lilies that bordered the walk. They turned from pure white to bright yellow, but bent their heads lower than ever, as though they were ashamed of the change that the touch of King Midas had wrought in them.

Before turning any more things into gold, the king sat down at the little table in the court that his slaves had laid for his meal. The parched wheat was fresh and crisp, and the grapes juicy and sweet. But when he tasted a grape, it became a very hard ball of gold in his mouth. This was very unpleasant. He laid the gold ball on the table and tried the parched wheat, only to have his mouth filled with hard yellow metal. Feeling as if he were choking, he took a sip of water, and at the touch of his lips even this became liquid gold.

Then all of King Midas's bright treasures began to look ugly to him, and his heart grew as heavy as if that, too, were turning to gold.

That night King Midas lay down under a gorgeous golden counterpane, with his head upon a pillow of solid gold; but he could not rest. Sleep would not come to him.

Now Midas had a young daughter, Little Marygold, upon whom he doted. The next morning, at breakfast, Marygold saw her father's distress as he tried, without success, to eat food before it turned to precious metal in his hand. Hoping to comfort him, Marygold ran from her chair and threw herself into her beloved father's arms. To Midas's great sorrow, he saw that his touch had turned his daughter, the love of his life, into a solid gold statue! Her rosy face, so full of affection, and the beautiful brown ringlets of her hair, all had been turned brilliant yellow. Even the tears that streaked her face as she sought to embrace her father had been turned to glittering gold drops on her cheeks.

Then Midas realized the folly of his wish for the Golden Touch, and he began to fear that he might accidentally turn his queen, his family, and all his kind friends into hard, golden statues. This would be more terrible than anything else that had resulted from his foolish wish. Poor Midas now saw that riches were not the most desirable of all things. He was cured forever of his love for gold.

While he wrung his hands in despair, he suddenly beheld a stranger standing near the door. Midas bent down his head, without speaking; for he recognized the same figure who had appeared to him the day before, in the treasure-room, and had bestowed on him this disastrous Golden Touch. The stranger's countenance still wore his mysterious smile.

"Well, friend Midas," said the stranger, "pray how do you succeed with the Golden Touch?"

Midas shook his head.

"I am very miserable," said he.

"Very miserable, indeed!" exclaimed the stranger. "And how happens that? Have I not faithfully kept my promise with you? Have you not everything that your heart desired?"

His touch had turned his daughter, the love of his life, into a solid gold statue!

"Gold is not everything," answered Midas. "And I have lost all that my heart really cared for."

"Ah! So you have made a discovery, since yesterday?" observed the stranger. "Let us see, then. Which of these two things do you think is really worth the most—the gift of the Golden Touch, or one cup of clear cold water?"

"O blessed water!" exclaimed Midas. "It will never moisten my parched throat again!"

"The Golden Touch," continued the stranger, "or a crust of bread?"

"A piece of bread," answered Midas, "is worth all the gold on earth!"

"The Golden Touch," asked the stranger, "or your own little Marygold, warm, soft, and loving as she was an hour ago?"

"Oh, my child, my dear child!" cried poor Midas, wringing his hands. "I would not have given that one small dimple in her chin for the power of changing this whole big earth into a solid lump of gold!"

"You are wiser than you were, King Midas!" said the stranger, looking seriously at him. "Your own heart,

I perceive, has not been entirely changed from flesh to gold. Were it so, your case would indeed be desperate. But you appear to be still capable of understanding that the commonest things, such as lie within everybody's grasp, are more valuable than the riches which so many mortals sigh and struggle after. Tell me, now, do you sincerely desire to rid yourself of this Golden Touch?"

"It is hateful to me!" replied Midas.

"Ah," said the stranger, "so you have gold enough at last. Very well. If you are sure that you do not wish to change anything more into gold, go and bathe in the spring where the river Pactolus rises. The pure water of that spring will wash away the Golden Touch and return all to as it was."

King Midas gladly obeyed, and became as free of the Golden Touch as when he was a boy watching the ants. And he returned home to find Little Marygold as warm and loving as she had been that morning. Midas cherished her love above all riches for all the remaining years of his life.

Bellerophon
and Pegasus

When the summer suns had scorched the plains and dried the rivers of Greece till hardly any green thing was left, there were meadows, high on the snowy sides of Mount Helicon, that were bright with soft young grasses, and dotted with flowers of every color.

In these meadows were the most glorious fountains, and the most beautiful of them was called the Fountain of Hippocrene. The waters of this fountain were the coolest and sweetest, and they had a wonderful magic. This fountain had not existed until one bright moonlit night when Pegasus, the winged horse, had struck the ground a sharp blow with his hoof, causing this fountain to gush forth. Pegasus came back occasionally to drink the waters of the Fountain of Hippocrene, and there was no place on earth where a plain mortal would be more likely to see him.

Now it happened one day that a certain young hero, named Bellerophon, came to Mount Helicon to look for Pegasus. He had been sent by a king to slay the Chimaera, a monstrous creature that was laying waste to the country. Bellerophon thought that, with the help of the winged horse, he might win an easy victory over any earth-born monster.

So, night after night, Bellerophon came to the Fountain of Hippocrene and watched for Pegasus. For a long time he could not see so much as a feather of the horse's glorious wings. Once or twice, when the moon was shining more brightly than usual, he did think that a shadow passed lightly over the grass, but when he looked up, there was nothing to be seen. Finally one night, after arriving at the spring much later than usual, he saw Pegasus careering gaily about the meadows. The horse's silvery wings were held high over his back, and his dainty

BELLEROPHON WOKE IN THE MORNING WITH THE FIRST SUNBEAMS
SHINING ON HIS FACE.

pink hoofs scarcely touched the ground. His whinnying was like the tremulous music of a flute; but when be saw Bellerophon, he spread his great white wings, and soared away up into the depths of the sky.

Catch Pegasus! Bellerophon saw that it was of no use to try, and gave it up. Then he lay down and slept on the soft grass of the meadow.

But people who slept near the Fountain of Hippocrene were apt to dream under its magic influence, and while Bellerophon slept, he dreamed that Minerva stood at his side with a golden bridle in her hand. In the dream she gave him the bridle, and then Pegasus came up to him, and bent his beautiful head to have it put on.

Bellerophon woke in the morning with the first sunbeams shining in his face, and found the golden bridle of his dream in his hands. The headpiece was set with jewels, and the whole bridle was so gorgeous that it seemed fit for so wonderful a horse as Pegasus. When night came, Bellerophon again waited for Pegasus.

He had hardly hidden himself in the nearby bushes when he saw a faint white speck in the sky that grew larger and larger, and soon took the shape of a winged horse. As the beautiful creature descended lower, he began to fly in great circles, lower and lower, till his hooves touched the meadow. Then he cantered up to Bellerophon, and held down his head for the jeweled bridle, just as he had done in Bellerophon's dream.

A more gentle horse than Pegasus never lived, nor one fonder of his rider. He seemed willing to take the owner of the bridle for his master, and was obedient to the rein. It was wonderful when he tried his wings. Up above the clouds he soared, with Bellerophon on his back. Who need fear the Chimaera now?

This Chimaera was a frightful monster with three heads—the head of a lion, the head of a goat, and the head of a snake. Its body was something like the shaggy body of a goat in the middle, and ended in a dragon's tail. When the creature was roused, it could belch out from its three cavernous mouths the fire and smoke that had turned the landscape ashen and desolate. The few people living near where it dwelled lived in constant terror of this creature.

PEGASUS, WITH ALL HIS WONDERFUL POWER OF FLIGHT, SPED
THROUGH THE AIR LIKE AN ARROW.

Obedient to Bellerophon's wish, Pegasus swooped straight down
to within striking distance of the Chimaera.

When Bellerophon felt that he had perfect control of Pegasus, he guided him straight toward the mountains where the Chimaera lived. Pegasus, with all his wonderful power of flight, sped through the air like an arrow, and in a very short time hovered above the cruel monster, which lay sprawling in the midst of the waste it had caused.

Obedient to Bellerophon's wish, Pegasus swooped straight down to within striking distance of the Chimaera. Then, a flash from Bellerophon's lance, and the goat's head hung limp. What a roar followed from the lion's head! All the air became filled with the sickening odor, and it began to grow dark with smoke. But Bellerophon and Pegasus were safe, high above the earth.

They waited till the monster was quiet again, then made another quick dash, and off went the lion's head. There was no roaring this time, and not so much fire and smoke, although the angry writhing of the creature was terrible to see. But the Chimaera could not follow Pegasus into the pure upper air.

Once more horse and rider dashed down, and the snake's head was severed from the Chimaera's body. Then the terrible fires burned themselves out, and that was the end of the Chimaera.

When the people of that country learned that the Chimaera was dead, they came back to their homes. Not long after, the hills, that had been so gray and desolate, were covered with vineyards and growing crops.

After this, Bellerophon, with the help of Pegasus, performed other wonderful feats, and became very famous. But one day, when he was foolish enough to try and fly Pegasus to Mount Olympus, Jupiter caused Pegasus to throw him. Blinded by the near sight of Olympus, and lamed by the fall, Bellerophon wandered about, for many years, an unhappy, helpless old man.

Hyacinthus and Apollo

Hyacinthus was a beautiful Greek boy who was greatly loved by Apollo. Apollo often laid aside his golden lyre and his arrows, and came down from Mount Olympus to join Hyacinthus in his boyish occupations. The two were often busy all day long, following the hunting-dogs over the mountains, or setting fishing nets in the river, or playing at various games.

Their favorite exercise was throwing the discus, a heavy metal plate scaled from the side of the body. One day Apollo threw the discus first, and sent it whirling high up among the clouds, for the god had great strength. It came down in a fine, strong curve, and Hyacinthus ran to pick it up. Then, as it fell on the hard earth, the discus bounded up again and struck the boy a cruel blow on his forehead.

Apollo turned as pale as Hyacinthus, but he could not undo what had been done. He could only hold his friend in his arms, and see his head droop like a lily on a broken stem, while the purple blood from his wound stained the earth and darkness fell on the young boy's eyes.

There was only one way by which Apollo could keep Hyacinthus alive, and that was to change him into a flower. So, quickly, he whispered over him certain words the gods knew, and Hyacinthus became a purple flower—a flower the color of the blood that had flowed from his forehead. As the flower unfolded, it showed a strange mark on its petals, which looked like the Greek words meaning *Woe! Woe!*

Apollo never forgot his friend; but sang about him to the accompaniment of his wonderful lyre till the name of Hyacinthus was known and loved all over Greece.

Darkness fell on the young boy's eyes.

Theseus and the Minotaur

Theseus and his mother, Aethra, lived at the foot of a great lonesome mountain, at a place called Troezen. One day, Aegeus, the father of Theseus, took Aethra up the mountainside to a great rock, under which he buried his sword and sandals. He then told Aethra that when Theseus was strong enough to lift this rock, she might let him take the sword and sandals and seek his father in Athens, where Aegeus sat on the throne.

At last the time came when Theseus had reached a man's full strength. Aethra led her son up the mountain and asked him to move the great rock. Theseus bent himself to the task, wrestling with the rock as though it were a human opponent. At last, the great rock stirred, and Theseus heaved it aside to reveal the treasures underneath. Taking the sword and sandals, as his mother instructed him, he put them on and set out on his journey to Athens.

Theseus had many adventures on his journey. He slew a robber named Periphetes, and took Periphetes' iron club with him. This he used to defeat Sinis, a giant whose pine-tree club proved no match for the iron club of Theseus. Other robbers and giants met similar fates at the hands of Theseus, among them Procrustes, a terrible robber who would invite strangers to sleep overnight in his house, and then cut off their heads or feet to fit the bed he gave them.

News spread of the heroic feats of Theseus, such that he was well-known by the time he reached Athens. In fact, only one man in all Athens knew nothing of his coming, and that man was his own father, Aegeus.

At this time Medea, a beautiful sorceress, was living in the king's palace. As she had a son whom she wished to place on the throne after King Aegeus was gone, she

The great rock stirred.

was fearful of the arrival of Theseus. By means of her knowledge of poisonous herbs she mixed a cup that would cause instant death to anyone who drank of it and, telling the king that the young stranger was a traitor who had plotted against his life, she bade him hand the cup to Theseus when he presented himself at the throne.

When he arrived, Theseus innocently raised the fatal cup to his lips, intending to drink to the king. Just then Aegeus noticed the sword Theseus carried, and recognized the carving on its ivory hilt as his own. Instantly, he struck the cup from the hand of Theseus, and welcomed the young man as a son.

Now, a long time before Theseus arrived in Athens, the oldest son of King Minos of Crete had been slain on Athenian soil. To avenge the prince's death, King Minos brought a great army against Athens, and forced the Athenians to pay him a tribute, every ninth year, of seven young men and seven maidens, chosen from among the noble families of Athens. It was whispered that the children of the tribute were then devoured by the Minotaur, a bloodthirsty creature with the body of a man and the head of a bull, which King Minos kept in a labyrinth near his palace. No one who entered the labyrinth had ever been known to come out again. The third time for paying the tribute had now come.

When Theseus heard of this, he vowed to kill the monstrous Minotaur, and offered himself, before the lots were drawn, as one of the seven young men. On the day appointed, the six other young men and the seven maidens drawn by lot boarded a ship outfitted with a sad black sail that the Cretans would recognize. Now that there was some hope of a happy outcome of the voyage, King Aegeus gave Theseus a white sail, and told him to hoist it instead of the black one for the homeward voyage, if he should succeed in killing the Minotaur.

When the children of the tribute arrived at Crete, Theseus told King Minos that he meant to kill the Minotaur. King Minos told the prince that if he could perform this task, he and all his companions might go free, and that nothing more should ever be said about the tribute. But he forbade Theseus to meet the Minotaur armed.

That night, Ariadne and Phaedra, the daughters of King Minos, took pity on Theseus and his companions and stole away to the dungeon where they had been put. The women led Theseus to the labyrinth and bade him to seek the Minotaur now, while he slept.

"The Minotaur's den is in the very heart of the labyrinth," said Ariadne. "The sound of his breathing will show you in what direction you must go. Here is a sword, and here is a ball of thread, by means of which, after you have killed the monster, you can find your way back." With these words she handed him the sword and the ball of thread, whose end she kept in her own hand.

Holding the sword in one hand and the thread in the other, Theseus entered the labyrinth. The interior was all broken up into narrow paths bordered by high walls, many of which ended in a blank wall. Theseus often had to retrace his steps. He could hear the heavy breathing more and more plainly, and knew that he was getting nearer to the den of the monster.

Ariadne and Phaedra waited at the gate a long time. The moon set behind the hills, and left only the light of the stars. Then they heard a great roar that shook the strong walls of the labyrinth. After this everything was still again. Ariadne felt the thread tighten, and in a moment more Theseus came out of the labyrinth, saying that he had slain the Minotaur.

The galley that had brought Theseus and his companions to Crete was still at the shore, and this made it possible to escape from King Minos before daylight. The sleeping youths and maidens in the dungeon were quickly roused, and the two princesses, knowing that Minos would be angry with them for their betrayal, accepted Theseus's invitation to go to Athens with him.

On their way back to Athens the young people stopped at the island of Naxos to rest. Very early the next morning they set sail, and started off again; but Ariadne, being fast asleep on a rock, was left behind. When Bacchus, the god of the vine, discovered her, he said, "Theseus should certainly have taken you to Athens. Considering all that you did to help him, he ought, at the very least, to have made you a queen. But never mind, you shall have a better crown than any he could

THEY NEVER ONCE THOUGHT WHETHER THEIR SAILS WERE BLACK,
OR WHITE, OR RAINBOW COLORED.

have given you." With these words the god placed a crown of nine bright stars on Ariadne's head. After this he persuaded the other gods to take her up into the sky, among themselves. There, in the northern sky, her crown still shines.

As the ship drew near Athens, the happy youths on board broke into song and dance. They never once thought whether their sails were black, or white, or rainbow colored, and Theseus forgot to hoist the white sail of victory. Poor King Aegeus, watching from the rock, saw the black sails, and thinking that his son was dead, threw himself into the sea and was drowned. So when the children of the tribute arrived safe in the harbor after such a dangerous journey, there was mourning instead of rejoicing.

After Theseus was made king, he brought his mother, Aethra, to Athens, and took good care of her for the rest of her life. He ruled wisely, and was kind to the poor and the unfortunate.

Philemon and Baucis

In a certain pleasant valley surrounded by low mountains, there was once a very wicked village. Strangers who had passed through this village on their travels complained bitterly that, if they were tired and hungry, and looked at the open doors of the houses, hoping for hospitality, it was only to see the doors slammed in their faces, and to hear the grinding of bolts. Some claimed to have been stoned and ill-treated in every possible way. It was no wonder that the news of these things reached the gods of Olympus.

One day, two strangers who were somewhat different from travelers in general, passed through the town. It was almost dark, and the night air felt sharp and frosty. The strangers knocked at door after door, without finding anyone who was willing to admit them, till they had tried every house but the last one in the village.

This last house stood out a little beyond the others, on the edge of a great swamp. It was a small cottage with only two rooms, and the roof was thatched with straw and with reeds from the swamp. Here lived Philemon and Baucis, an old couple who were not at all like the rest of the people in the village. They would never have thought of bolting their doors when they saw strangers coming. Instead, they opened their doors, and invited these two in.

The two rooms inside were almost bare of furniture. But Philemon and Baucis, poor as they were, made the strangers welcome to the best of all they had. Baucis drew the ashes from the fire, which had been kept from the day before, brought in firewood, and soon had it crackling under a small kettle. While the water was heating, she brought vegetables from her little garden, and sat down to strip off the leaves.

Meanwhile, Philemon lifted down a side of bacon which hung on a beam overhead, and cut off a piece for Baucis to cook.

Then Baucis brought out a rickety table, and placed upon it a few figs that had grown in her own garden, a brown loaf, and a pitcher of fresh, cold milk. When the bacon and the vegetables were done, she roasted some fresh eggs in the embers. The dinner was now ready, and the strangers were invited to seat themselves at the table.

If Philemon and Baucis had been alone, their dinner would have consisted of nothing more than the brown bread and the milk, with perhaps a small scrap of bacon. But Baucis thought that the strangers must be tired and hungry, and it seemed to her that it was her duty to show them such hospitality as her small means would allow.

As the four began to eat the meal, a very strange thing happened. The pitcher of milk, as it was passed round the table from one to another, was always full to the brim, no matter how much had just been drunk.

When Philemon and Baucis saw this, they were frightened. They had heard of such things happening, when people had been entertaining the gods, unaware. Looking at their guests more closely, they saw that the taller one certainly had a majestic air. The other had a face whose expression was constantly changing, and there was a look of mischief in his bright eyes.

The first thought of both of the old people, now, was that they had not done enough for such guests. Baucis jumped up from her chair, and ran out to catch the goose—the only thing that she and Philemon had left—intending to cook that, too. Philemon tried to help her, but neither of the old people could see very well, and they could not catch the goose. At last it ran into the cottage and straight up to the two strange guests, who said it should not be killed.

Then the guests told Philemon and Baucis that they were the gods Jupiter and Mercury, and why they had come to the village. They had heard the complaints of the travelers who had been so badly used, and had come to see whether the people of that village really were so wicked. They had found it all too true, and now, they said, these people must be punished.

THE PITCHER OF MILK, AS IT WAS PASSED ROUND THE TABLE FROM
ONE TO ANOTHER, WAS ALWAYS FULL TO THE BRIM.

Then they told the old couple, who had shown kindness and generosity where the other villagers had shown wickedness, to follow them up the mountainside. There was a full moon, and Philemon and Baucis could see almost as clearly as their old eyes would let them see in the daytime. When they had nearly reached the top of the mountain, Jupiter told them to turn and look back at the village. The houses were slowly sinking out of sight, and presently a lake took their place, and looked as though no village had ever been there.

Then a change came over the house of Philemon and Baucis. The thatched roof began to turn yellow, like gold, while the sides grew white, and it became a marble temple, with a golden roof. Jupiter told Philemon and Baucis to wish for whatever they liked, and their wish should be granted. The two old people could think of nothing better than that they might die at exactly the same moment, so that neither one should be left to mourn the other. Jupiter and Mercury then vanished and the old people went back down the mountain, and became priest and priestess in the temple, where

THE WEARY, AND THE HUNGRY, AND THE THIRSTY USED TO REPOSE
THEMSELVES AND DRINK ABUNDANTLY OUT OF THE MIRACULOUS PITCHER.

they lived happily for many years. The miraculous pitcher remained in their possession, and they shared it generously with those who visited the temple.

One morning early, a long, long time afterward, some peasants came up to the temple with a present of new-laid eggs for the old priest and priestess. Imagine their astonishment when, on coming near the temple, they saw two grand old trees, an oak and a lime, standing just in front of the temple doors, where no tree had ever stood before. This was a marvel to them. When they came to look for Philemon and Baucis, they could not find them, and the two old people were never seen in that country again. But the two trees stood there for many, many centuries, even after the temple had grown old and fallen to ruin. And the miraculous pitcher remained forever in their shade. The weary, and the hungry, and the thirsty used to repose themselves and drink abundantly out of the miraculous pitcher. And travelers who rested in the hospitable shade of the trees used to tell each other the story of the wicked villagers, and of the kindness of Philemon and Baucis.

Pygmalion and Galatea

In days when the world was young and the gods walked the earth, there reigned over the island of Cyprus a sculptor-king named Pygmalion, whose only passion was his art. He had no interest in women, whom he scorned for distracting men from their work. From great rough blocks of marble he would sculpt the most perfect semblances of men, and of women, and of everything that seemed to him the most beautiful and the most worth preserving.

One day, as he chipped and chiseled, there came to him the image of a beautiful woman imprisoned in the stone. Her form and features all were perfect, and he knew that he had to set her free. At last came the day when he felt that one more chisel stroke would be too many, and he laid his chisel aside and gazed at her beauty. Then Pygmalion covered his eyes.

Day by day his love for this woman of his own creation grew, and pushed all other concerns from his mind. His hands grew idle. He would dream dreams of his marble woman in which she became a woman of warm flesh and blood. But when he returned to his studio he would find her still made of stone and, heartbroken, he would kiss her cold lips and hands.

To his beloved statue he gave the name Galatea. And everywhere he went, he heard her name called out to him: by the silver stars in the still of the night; in the winds that blew across the sands; in the white surf that broke upon the rocks at the oceanside. So great was his love for her that he decked a couch with the most expensive furs and the softest pillows that he might lay her down upon it.

So time wore on, and the festival of Aphrodite drew near. As the leader of his people, Pygmalion dutifully participated in all of the ceremonies, and at last found

Then Pygmalion covered his eyes.

himself alone by the altar to pray. Never before had his words faltered as he prayed, but on this day he spoke not as a sculptor-king, but as a lovelorn man.

"Oh, Aphrodite!" he implored, "you who can do all things. I pray you, give me one like my Galatea for my wife!" Though he dared not ask for Galatea, Aphrodite knew well the words he would have uttered, and smiled to think how Pygmalion had changed. In token that his prayer was answered, she made the flames on the altar shoot up in a fiery point three times. Pygmalion went home, scarcely daring to hope that his wish had been granted.

The shadows of evening were falling as he entered the room that he had made sacred to Galatea. There on the couch she lay, and it seemed as though she met his eyes with her own; that she smiled at him in welcome. He knelt by her side, and made to kiss her cold marble lips, as he had so many times before. But now it seemed that those lips were as warm as his own! He felt one of her hard marble hands, and found them no longer stiff to his touch. He laid his fingers gently on her marble hair,

and found it soft and wavy. Pygmalion kissed her lips—
and then did Galatea open her eyes as wide as pools of a
dark mountain stream on which the sun is shining, and
gaze with timid gladness into his own.

We know little more of Pygmalion and Galatea:
only that their lives were happy, and that to them was
born a son, named Paphos, from whom the city sacred
to Aphrodite took its name. We can only guess that
Aphrodite may have smiled sometimes to look down on
Pygmalion, the adoring servant of the woman that his
own hands had first designed.

ECHO OFTEN SAW NARCISSUS, AND SHE ADMIRED HIM VERY MUCH.

Echo and Narcissus

Echo was a nymph who talked too much. She was very fond of having the last word. One day she spoke rudely to the great Juno, who said that for this offense Echo should never use her voice again, unless to repeat what she had just heard.

This was almost as bad as if Juno had changed her into a parrot! Echo was very much ashamed, and hid herself in the forest.

Narcissus, a young man who had hair as yellow as gold and eyes as blue as the sky, used to hunt in the forest where Echo was hiding. As she peeped out shyly from some cave or from behind a great tree, Echo often saw Narcissus, and she admired him very much.

One day Narcissus became separated from his friends, and hearing something rustle among the leaves, he called out, "Who's here?"

"Here," answered Echo.

"Here I am. Come!" said Narcissus.

"I am come," said Echo; and, as she spoke, she came out from among the trees.

When Narcissus saw a stranger, instead of one of his friends as he had expected, he looked surprised and walked quickly away.

After this, Echo never allowed herself to be seen again, and in time she faded away till she became only a voice.

This voice was heard for many, many years in forests and among mountains, particularly in caves. In their solitary walks, hunters often heard it. Sometimes it mocked the barking of their dogs; sometimes it repeated their own last words. It always had a mournful sound, and seemed to make lonely places more lonely still.

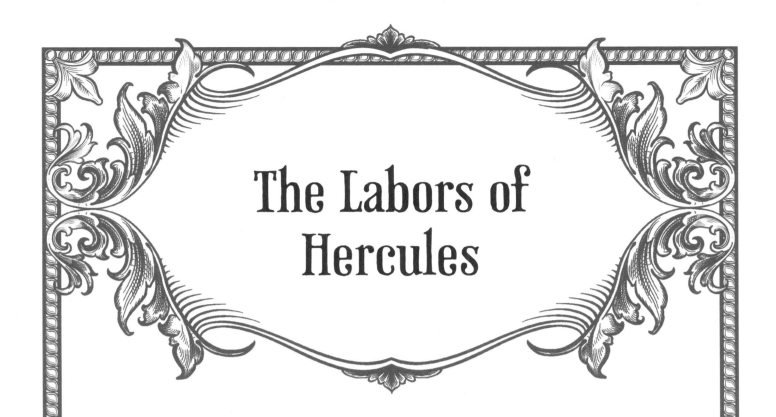

The Labors of Hercules

Among all the heroes about whom the old Greek harpers used to sing, there was one who was celebrated more than the rest. This was Hercules. He was loved by the Greeks better than any of their other heroes, because he was stronger and braver than any of the others.

As a boy, Hercules was carefully trained in all the things that Greek boys were accustomed to learn. He was taught his letters, how to play the lyre, and how to shoot with the bow and arrow. He was taught by his father, Amphitryon, how to ride standing in his chariot. He also learned how to box, wrestle, throw the discus, and fight with the lance and shield. During the day he was always at his father's side, and at night his bed, which was covered with a lion's skin, stood near that of his father.

When Hercules was grown up, he presented himself as ready for any task at the court of King Eurystheus, in Mycenae. There was nothing the Greeks admired more than great bodily strength, and Hercules was already remarkable for his broad shoulders, and the large muscles of his arms. Eurystheus, who was Hercules' older cousin, had always been weak and sickly.

So when Hercules stood before him for the first time, King Eurystheus looked at his strong young cousin, and felt his courage sink at the difference between them. Angered, he resolved to set Hercules the hardest and most dangerous tasks that he could possibly imagine before he would grant Hercules freedom from service.

These tasks which Hercules performed for King Eurystheus became famous in after days, and were called the Twelve Labors of Hercules. Each one was a little harder than the last, and carried Hercules a little farther from home and a little nearer to the unknown western land, till in the twelfth he even reached the gates of Hades, where Pluto reigned.

For his first labor, Hercules strangled a savage tiger that had preyed upon the people of Nemea. Next, he killed the hydra, a monster that grew two new heads for each head he cut off. He also captured a bear, a bull, a pair of war-horses, a golden-horned stag sacred to the goddess Diana, and a herd of cattle owned by a six-legged giant with three heads and three bodies. He rid a forest of evil birds, stole a girdle given by the god Mars to the warrior Amazon women, and overpowered Cerberus, the three-headed dog who guards the underworld, to bring him to Eurystheus's court. For one of his hardest labors, Hercules cleaned a huge stable for cattle by diverting a river through it.

Among Hercules' most challenging labors was the retrieval of three golden apples from the Garden of the Hesperides, in a country beyond the sunset.

Although all had heard of this famous garden, no one at Mycenae could tell Hercules where to find it.

Some said it was far to the north, others that it was far to the west.

So Hercules started out, and walked in a northwesterly direction, until he reached the river's edge. There he found the river-nymphs playing among the rocks. When he asked them where he might find the Garden of the Hesperides, they tried to convince him how dangerous it would be to go there. He sat down on the grass and told them the story of his life, and the many hard labors that he had already performed.

When he told them his name was Hercules, they replied, "We had already guessed it; for your wonderful deeds are known all over the world. We do no think it strange any longer that you should set out in your quest of the golden apples of the Hesperides."

They told him that Nereus, the sea-god, knew where to find the Garden of the Hesperides, but would never tell the secret unless he were forced to do so. They told him also that, without any fear of what might happen, he must seize Nereus, and hold him fast till he gave the desired information. "Do not be astonished at anything

He sat down on the grass, and told them the story of his life.

He saw the poor old sea-god sleeping soundly.

that may happen. Only hold him tight, and he will tell you what you wish to know."

Thanking the nymphs for their kindness, Hercules followed the river down to the place where it flowed into the sea. Then he lay in wait behind some rocks, till the sun went down and the moon came up.

Presently, a queer little old man came up out of the water, and set about making himself comfortable for a nap on shore. The old man had webbed hands and feet, and his long hair and beard had the appearance of a tangle of seaweed. Hercules knew at once that this was Nereus; and as soon as he saw the poor old sea-god sleeping soundly, he ran out and seized him, as the nymphs had said he must.

All at once he found that he was holding a struggling stag; then the stag became a sea-bird, screaming to get free; the sea-bird changed to a fierce three-headed dog; the three-headed dog took the form of the three-headed giant, Geryon, whom Hercules had slain during of his earlier labors; next Geryon changed to a monstrous snake. All this time Hercules held on tighter and tighter.

At last, Nereus, seeing that he could not frighten Hercules into letting him go, took his proper shape again and asked him what he wanted.

Hercules replied that he only wanted to know how to get three of the golden apples which grew in the Garden of the Hesperides. "You must go on, thus and thus," said Nereus, after taking the points of a compass, "till you come in sight of a tall giant who holds up the world. That giant's name is Atlas, and if he is in good humor, he will tell you exactly where the Garden of the Hesperides lies."

So Hercules followed the directions given him by Nereus. Almost as soon as he had touched the shore he had been directed to, he was attacked by a terrible earth-born giant, called Antaeus. This was a very difficult giant to conquer. The secret of his wonderful strength was that his mother, Gaea, the goddess of the earth, made him stronger than ever, each time that he touched the ground. Thus, the harder that Hercules hit the giant with his club and knocked him to the ground, the stronger Antaeus was when he arose. But Hercules, knowing how Gaea helped him, held Antaeus high above the earth, and squeezed and squeezed his body so strongly that, finally, he squeezed all of Antaeus's strength out of his body.

When his fight with Antaeus was over, Hercules lay down on the ground and went to sleep. He soon awoke, feeling as if he were being stung by a thousand insects. Sitting up, and rubbing his eyes, what should he see but a multitude of tiny people no larger than bumble-bees, who, while he was asleep, had been climbing over his body, and attacking him with their little bows and arrows. These were the Pygmies, who were earth-born people like Antaeus, as tiny as he was giant.

The Pygmies had only one trouble in the world, and that was the flock of cranes that lived nearby. They were constantly at war with the cranes, and often went into battle against them mounted on the backs of squirrels, or rabbits, or rats, armed with small bows and arrows or spears. If, during battle, a pygmy managed to pluck out a crane's tail-feather, it was considered a prize trophy. Once, a pygmy soldier was made king of the pygmy nation for no other feat than bringing home such a feather.

The Pygmies had witnessed the destruction of their brother, Antaeus, and when they saw Hercules preparing to take his nap, they determined that they could not let him leave their land unharmed. So the leader of the Pygmies ordered that a thousand pygmy archers draw their bows ready against Hercules. The same number were ordered to clamber upon the sleeping Hercules, which proved difficult for those who schemed to plug up his mouth and nose, as the giant's breath rushed out of his nose with the force of a hurricane whirlwind, blowing them away as fast as they came nigh.

"What's all this?" cried Hercules, when he was awakened by the sting of the pygmy arrows.

"Villain!" shouted the Pygmies. "You have slain Antaeus, our brother. We declare war against you."

"Upon my word," cried Hercules, "I thought I had seen wonders before today—hydras with heads, stags with golden horns, six-legged men, three-headed dogs, and who knows what besides. But here," he said, plucking up one of the pygmy soldiers between his fingers and holding him in the palm of his hand, "stands

THEY WERE CONSTANTLY AT WAR WITH THE CRANES.

THE GIANT'S BREATH RUSHED OUT OF HIS NOSE WITH THE FORCE
OF A HURRICANE WHIRLWIND.

a wonder that outdoes them all." Hercules laughed heartily at their warfare, and then he tied a few of them into a corner of his lion's skin, to take back as playthings for the children of Eurystheus.

And so Hercules wandered on until he came upon a sight even more marvelous than all of his other labors. It was a giant as tall as a mountain. The clouds rested about his waist like a girdle, and hung like a beard from his chin. Upon his back, he appeared to be holding up the very sky itself.

Looking down from his great height, the giant saw Hercules, and called out in a voice that bellowed like thunder, "What are you at my feet? And why do you come here?"

"I am Hercules," cried the hero. "Can you show me the way to the Garden of the Hesperides? I wish to bring back three of its golden apples."

"Nobody but myself can go to this garden," said Atlas. "If it were not for this business of having to hold up the sky, I would cross the sea in half a dozen steps and gather the apples for you."

"Well then," said Hercules. "I shall climb the mountain behind you there and relieve you of your burden, so that you can collect the apples for me." Without any more words, Hercules ascended the mountain, and Atlas shifted the sky from his shoulders to those of Hercules.

When Atlas came back with the apples, as he did shortly, he offered to carry them to Eurystheus himself, if Hercules would only hold up the world a little longer. Really, though, he meant that Hercules should continue to hold up the sky, forever.

But Hercules saw through the trick, and matched it with another. He thanked Atlas, and asked him to take the world again, for a moment, while he found a pad which would make the weight much easier to bear. So Atlas took the world again. Then Hercules took the apples, and although Atlas shouted to him to come back, he was soon beyond the sound of the giant's voice, and well on his way to Mycenae and his next adventure.

I SHALL CLIMB THE MOUNTAIN BEHIND YOU THERE AND RELIEVE YOU
OF YOUR BURDEN.

She checked her hounds and stood beside the boy.

Endymion's Sleep

Endymion was a young shepherd who led his flocks high up on the sides of Mount Latmus and let them browse on the rich pasturage along the margins of its snow-fed streams. He loved the pure mountain air, and the stillness of the higher slopes, which was broken only by the tinkle of his sheep-bells, or the song of birds. There he dreamed his days away, while his sheep and goats were feeding; or, at night, he leaned his head on a log or a mossy stone and slept with the flock.

Selene, the moon-goddess, loved to visit Mount Latmus with her hounds; in fact, the mountain belonged to her. It was her influence that made everything there so quiet and beautiful. One night, when she had stolen down from her place in the sky for a walk through one of the flowery meadows of Mount Latmus, she found Endymion there asleep. She checked her hounds and stood beside the boy.

The shepherd looked as beautiful as any flower on the mountain, or as the swans which were floating in the lake nearby, with their heads tucked under their wings. If it had not been for his regular breathing, Selene would have believed that she stood looking at a marble statue. There, at a little distance, lay his sheep and goats, unguarded, and liable to be attacked by wild beasts. Oh, Endymion was a very careless shepherd! That was the effect of the air on Mount Latmus.

Selene knew that it was the wonderful air of her mountain which had made the shepherd heedless, as well as beautiful; therefore, she stayed by his flock all night and watched it herself.

She came the next night, and the next, and for many nights, to gaze at the sleeper, and to watch the unguarded flock. One morning, when she returned to the sky, she looked so pale from her watching that Jupiter asked her where she had been, and she described the beautiful shepherd she had found on her mountain, and confessed that she had been guarding his sheep.

Then she begged of Jupiter that since Endymion was so very, very beautiful he might always look as she had seen him in his sleep, instead of growing old as other mortals must. Jupiter answered, "Even the gods cannot give to mortals everlasting youth and beauty without giving them also everlasting sleep; but Endymion shall sleep forever and be forever young."

So there, in a cave, on Mount Latmus, Endymion sleeps on to this day; and his wonderful beauty has not faded in the smallest degree, but is a joy still to all who can climb those lofty heights.

Orpheus and Eurydice

Orpheus, the son of Apollo, was a wonderful musician. He had a lyre of his own, and learned to play on it when he was very young. This lyre was not quite as famous as Apollo's golden lyre, but it could produce marvelous music.

Orpheus often went to a lonely place, outside of the village, where he would sit on the rocks and play all day long. When he went to this place to play, all of the animals and birds in the fields and forest gathered around him. Lions, bears, wolves, foxes, eagles, hawks, owls, squirrels, little field-mice, and many other creatures were in the audience. Even the trees in the grove nearby tore themselves up by the roots, and came and stood in the circle around Orpheus, so that they could hear better. Their branches cast a pleasant shade over Orpheus and his listeners, keeping off the hot rays of the afternoon sun.

The nymphs of the valley soon made friends with Orpheus, and when he had grown to be a man, one of them, named Eurydice, became his wife.

One day, as Eurydice was running carelessly through the meadows, she stepped on a snake that sometimes listened to her husband's music. Although the snake was always gentle when under the influence of the magical music of Orpheus, he was not so at other times, and he turned and bit Eurydice on the ankle. The bite proved fatal, sending Eurydice down to the dark underworld, where Pluto was king and Proserpine his queen.

When Orpheus came back to the meadows, he could not find Eurydice. Her sister nymphs joined him in his search, and everywhere the hills echoed their calls of "Eurydice, Eurydice!" But there was no answer.

Orpheus could not bear to give up Eurydice for lost. After he had looked everywhere on earth without finding her, he knew that she must be trapped in the underworld. He made up his mind that he would go down and play his lyre before King Pluto, hoping that he might perhaps persuade Pluto and Proserpine to let her come back to the sunny valley again.

So he went down to Pluto's kingdom until he came to a high dark gateway. It was barred with iron bars, and bolted and locked. And in front of this great gateway there sat Cerberus, a monstrous dog with three heads, and six eyes, and three mouths, who guarded the entrance to the underworld. When Cerberus saw Orpheus, he roared terribly and prepared to pounce upon him and tear him to pieces. But Orpheus only took his lyre and began to play it, and the sweet music was so soothing that it lulled Cerberus to sleep. When Orpheus passed by him and came up to the gate, he found that his beautiful music had unlocked it.

On he went until he entered the throne room of King Pluto, and there he played such a sweet, sad song that tears came to the eyes of all who heard it. Even Pluto, whom men thought very hard-hearted, could not help feeling sorry for Orpheus.

When the song was over, Orpheus implored that Eurydice might be allowed to return with him to the upper world, saying that he could not return without her. Pluto consented to let her go on one condition: that Orpheus have faith to believe that Eurydice was following him, and not look back to see her until he reached the upper world.

So Orpheus started back again, playing softly on his lyre. The music was not sad now. You would have thought that the dawn was coming, and that young birds were just waking in their nests. And he passed through the dark gateway, and Cerberus did not bark or growl, for he remembered the music that Orpheus had made, and knew that Orpheus would not have been allowed to come back had Pluto not wished it. In the darkness (for it is always dark in the underworld), Eurydice was following; but Orpheus could not be sure of this. He slowly climbed the steep path over the rocks, back to the world of light and warmth. Just as he had almost reached that familiar world—just as he could feel the fresh air from the sea on his forehead, and could see the glimmer

ORPHEUS SAW EURYDICE FADING AWAY AND SINKING DOWN
INTO THE UNDERWORLD.

of a sunbeam reflected on the rocks—he felt all at once that Eurydice was not there. The thought flashed into his mind that King Pluto might have deceived him, and he turned his head—

By the dim light which was beginning to break over his path, Orpheus saw Eurydice fading away and sinking down into the underworld. Her arms were stretched out toward him, but she could not follow him any farther. "Oh, Orpheus," she cried, "why did you look back? How dearly I love you and how glad I would have been to be with you again. But now I must go back because you have broken your promise to the king. I must not kiss you, or say how much I love you."

Oh, if only he had not looked back! Eurydice was lost indeed now. Orpheus knew that it would be of no use to try again to bring her to the upper world. He did not go back to the pleasant valley in which he had grown up, but went to live on a lonely mountain, where he spent all his days in grieving for Eurydice.

The music that came from his lyre was so sad, now, that it would have broken anyone's heart to hear it.

When the wind blew from the north, the people who lived at the foot of the mountain could faintly hear the mournful, wailing sound of the lyre. It came down the mountain to them, almost every day, for seven months, and then the north wind did not bring them those strains any more.

No one knows whatever became of Orpheus. His lyre floated down the river Hebrus, and then out to sea, sending out sweet sounds as it went, with the rise and fall of the water. One day, when the waves ran high, it was cast up on the shore at the island of Lesbos. There it remained, till it was all overgrown with vines and flowers, and half-buried under falling leaves. The nightingales were said to sing more sweetly on that island than in any other place.

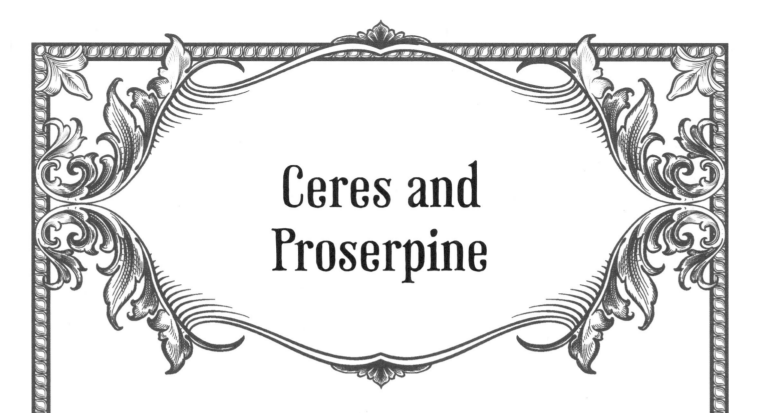

Ceres and Proserpine

Ceres, the Earth-Mother, and her daughter, Proserpine, lived in the valley of Enna. The valley owed its beauty to the presence of Ceres, and the magnificence of the plants that covered the whole island was due to her influence; for she was the goddess of all that grows out of the earth, and knew the secret of the springing wheat and the ripening fruits.

On a day when Ceres had to leave home to help hasten the harvest, she allowed Proserpine to go outside to play.

Wandering through the fields, what should Proserpine see but a beautiful flower that made her forget everything else. This flower was of gigantic size, and its one flower-stalk held at least a hundred blossoms. Its fragrance was so powerful that it perfumed the entire island.

No sooner had she stooped to pluck this beautiful blossom than the black soil around the plant loosened, and a great black cavern appeared. From out of its depths sprang four magnificent black horses, drawing a golden chariot. In the chariot sat a king with the gloomiest face Proserpine had ever seen. When he saw Proserpine, he snatched her from the ground and drove his chariot away at a furious rate.

Though far away, Ceres heard Proserpine's screams for help and rushed to where she had last seen her daughter. All that she found were a few roses scattered on the ground, and no sign of the magnificent flower that had tempted Proserpine.

Ceres searched night and day for her beloved Proserpine. On the tenth night, when it was nearly morning, she met the goddess Hecate, who told Ceres how she had heard Proserpine scream, and had heard the sound of wheels, but had seen nothing. Then she went with the goddess to ask Helios, the sun-god, whether he had seen what happened that day, for the sun-god travels around the whole world, and must see everything. Indeed, he had: Helios told Ceres that Pluto, the king of the underworld, had stolen her daughter and had carried her away to live with him in his dark palace.

When Ceres heard this, she knew that Proserpine was lost to her, and she hid herself in the dark places of the earth. She liked to keep away from the earth's people as well as from the gods, for wherever she went, she was sure to see some happy mother with her children around her, and the sight made her feel very lonely. She sometimes envied the poorest peasants, or even the little bird-mothers in the trees.

Now all this time while Ceres had been mourning for her lost Proserpine, she had neglected to look after the little seeds that lay in the brown earth. The consequence was that these little seeds could not sprout and grow; therefore there was no grain to be ground into flour for bread. Not only the seeds, but all growing things missed the care of Mother Ceres. The grass turned brown and withered away, the trees in the olive orchards dropped their leaves, and the little birds all flew away to a distant country. Even the sheep that fed among the water-springs in the valley of Enna grew so thin that it was pitiful to see them.

Jupiter saw that without Ceres, the Great Mother, there could be no life on the earth. In time, all men and animals would die for lack of food. He therefore told Iris to set up her rainbow-bridge in the sky, and to go quickly down to the dark cave where Ceres mourned for Proserpine, that she might persuade the goddess to forget her sorrow, and go back to the fields, where she was so much needed.

Iris found Ceres sitting in a corner of her cave, among the shadows, wrapped in dark blue draperies that made her almost invisible. The coming of Iris lighted up every part of the cave and set beautiful colors dancing everywhere, but it did not make Ceres smile.

After this, Jupiter sent the gods, one after another, down to the cave; but none of them could comfort the Earth-mother. She still mourned.

Then Jupiter sent Mercury down into Pluto's kingdom to see whether he could not persuade that grim king to let Proserpine return to her mother. When Mercury told his errand to Pluto, Proserpine jumped up from her throne, eager to see her mother again. Pluto, seeing how glad she was, could not withhold his consent. So he ordered the black horses and the golden chariot brought out to take her back. But before Proserpine sprang to the chariot's seat, Pluto craftily asked her if she would not like to eat one of the pomegranates that grew in his garden.

One of Pluto's servants brought the pomegranate to Proserpine on a silver tray, and she tasted the fruit, taking just six seeds. Then the black horses swiftly carried Mercury and herself into the upper world, and straight to the cave where Ceres sat.

What a change! How quickly Ceres ran out of the cave, when she heard her daughter's voice! No more mourning in shadowy places for her, now!

Proserpine told her mother everything—how she had found the wonderful flower, how the earth had

ONE OF PLUTO'S SERVANTS BROUGHT THE POMEGRANATE TO
PROSERPINE ON A SILVER TRAY.

opened, allowing King Pluto's horses to spring out, and how the dark king had snatched her away.

"My dear child," Ceres anxiously inquired, "have you eaten anything since you have been in the underworld?"

Proserpine confessed that she had eaten the six pomegranate seeds. At that, Ceres beat her breast in despair, and then appealed to Jupiter. He said that Proserpine should spend six months of every year with her mother, but would have to pass the other six—one for each pomegranate seed she ate—in the underworld with Pluto.

So Ceres went back to her beautiful valley of Enna, and to her work in the fields. The little brown seeds that had lain asleep so long sprouted up and grew; the fountains sent up their waters; the brown grass on the hills became green; the olive trees and the grape-vines put out new leaves; the lambs and the kids skipped about more gaily than ever; and all the hosts of little birds came back with the crane of Ceres to lead them.

During the six months that Proserpine was with her, Ceres went about again among the peasants, standing near the men while they were threshing the grain, helping the women to bake their bread, and having care over everything that went on. When the time came for Proserpine to go back to King Pluto, Ceres sat among the shadows in the cave, as she had done before, and the world turned gray and withered.

All nature slept for a while; but the peasants had no fear now, for they knew that Proserpine would surely come back, and that the great Earth-Mother would then care for her children again.

Cupid and Psyche

There once was a king who had three daughters, all of whom were known far and wide for their beauty. The most beautiful of all was the youngest, Psyche. When this young princess went into the temples, many people mistook her for the goddess Venus herself, and offered her the garlands which they had brought for the goddess of love and beauty.

Venus was much vexed by this, and determined to revenge herself on poor Psyche, who was in no way to blame. One day she told her son Cupid, the god of love, to wound Psyche with one of his golden-pointed arrows, and make her fall in love with the most wretched beggar that could be found.

Cupid took his arrows and went down to the earth to do his mother's bidding. As soon as he saw Psyche, he was so startled by her beauty that he wounded himself with his own arrow, and fell in love with Psyche.

Although Psyche was the most beautiful of the three sisters, her two older sisters had wed kings' sons long before. No man had asked for the hand of Psyche, and the king suspected that this had to do with the wrath of Venus. He inquired of the oracle what he should do, and these are the words she spoke to him:

> Dress thy daughter like a bride,
> Lead her up the mountainside,
> There an unknown winged foe,
> Feared by all who dwell below,
> And even by the gods above,
> Will claim her, as a hawk the dove.

The king was overcome with grief to hear this, but he did not dare to disobey. So one night he had one of Psyche's maids of honor dress her in wedding garments, and a long procession of her father's people escorted her to an exposed rock at the top of a high mountain, where they left her alone in the darkness.

Psyche sat on a rock, weeping in fear that at any moment she might hear the rushing wings of some dragon, and feel his claws and teeth. Instead, she felt the cool breath and the downy wings of Zephyrus, the west wind, who lifted her gently from the rock, then puffed out his cheeks, and blew her down into a beautiful green valley, where he laid her softly on a bank of violets.

When she woke in the morning, she saw a beautiful grove of tall trees, and in that grove a most wonderful palace, with a fountain in front of it. The great arches of the roof were supported by golden columns, and the walls were covered with silver carvings. The floor was a mosaic of precious stones of all colors.

Psyche timidly walked through the doors, and wandered through the great rooms, each of which seemed more splendid than the last. She could see no one, but once or twice thought she heard low voices, as though the fairies were talking to one another.

Presently, she opened the door of a room, where a table was laid ready for a feast. Only one guest was expected, though, for there was but one chair and one place setting. Psyche, seated herself in the chair, and the invisible fairies of the palace waited on her. After the last dish had been whisked away by unseen hands, she heard music—a chorus of singing voices, and then a single voice, accompanied by a lyre, which seemed to play of itself.

Psyche grew fearful as night came on, and she heard in the darkness the sound of wings, and footsteps coming down the great hall toward her. But then a sweet, musical voice said to her: "Beautiful Psyche, this palace and all it holds is yours, if you will consent to live here and be my wife. The voices you have heard are the voices of your handmaidens, who will obey any commands that you give them. Every night I will spend here with you; but before day comes, I must fly away. Do not ask to see my face, or to know who I am. Only trust me; I ask nothing more."

And so Psyche dwelled in splendor in the palace. Her mysterious lover visited her every night, and each night she looked forward to his coming.

PSYCHE TIMIDLY WALKED THROUGH THE DOORS, AND WANDERED
THROUGH THE GREAT ROOMS.

One day, while she was gathering roses within sight of the rock from which Zephyrus had blown her into the valley, she saw her two sisters beating their breasts and crying out as though mourning for the dead. When she heard them call her name, she knew that her sisters must think her dead.

That night, when her lover came to her, Psyche asked him if she might not see her sisters, and let them know that she was alive and happy. Though reluctant, he gave his consent. But he warned her not to answer any questions they might ask about him. And he reminded her that if she ever tried to see him face-to-face, he should be forced to fly away, and that the palace would vanish.

The next day Zephyrus brought Psyche's sisters into the valley as they had brought her before. When the spiteful pair saw their sister's superior fortune, they hatched a plan to destroy her happiness, and told her that the owner of the palace must be a horrible winged serpent, the nameless monster prophesied by the oracle, which was why she never was allowed her to look upon him.

When they had gone, poor Psyche found herself beset by questions that she could not answer. Why was her lover so anxious to be hidden in the darkness? Why did he fear her sisters' visit? Why did he have wings? Why did she sometimes hear a sound like that of a serpent gliding across the marble floors?

That night, while her lover lay sleeping, Psyche snuck into his room with a lighted lamp. There she saw no scaly serpent, but Cupid himself, his hair in golden curls and his delicate snow-white wings folded peacefully in sleep. Taking one of his arrows, Psyche pricked her finger with its tip, and felt the fullness of her love for him. But a drop of hot oil from the lamp fell on his shoulder, wounding him. Startled awake, Cupid quickly flew away and the palace around her vanished.

Then Psyche began a long search for her lost Cupid, which finally brought her to Venus. Venus was angry, and imposed nearly impossible tasks as punishment before she would let Psyche see Cupid again.

Venus charged Psyche with separating a large pile of mixed seeds into piles of the individual grains, retrieving the golden wool of a flock of fierce sheep, and filling a crystal vase with water from the dragon-guarded Fountain of Forgetfulness. All of these tasks Psyche accomplished with the assistance of plants and animals, who helped her for the sake of love.

For the last task, Venus commanded Psyche to travel to the underworld and bring back some of Proserpine's beauty. Venus gave Psyche a box in which to carry it, and forbade Psyche to look inside the box. Psyche did as she was told but, thinking to take some of Proserpine's beauty for herself, she disobeyed Venus and lifted the box's lid.

Something invisible rushed out of the box, and Psyche fell into a deep sleep. She might never have waked again if Cupid, his wounds healed, had not passed by and seen her. The god awakened her tenderly, then sent her with the box back to his mother, while he flew to Mount Olympus and laid his case before Jupiter.

The king of the gods, after hearing the story, said that Psyche should be made immortal, and should become the bride of Cupid. Mercury was sent to bring Psyche up to Mount Olympus, and at a feast in her honor Jupiter himself handed her the cup of sacred nectar. Psyche drank from the golden cup, and straightaway two beautiful butterfly-like wings sprang from her shoulders, and she became like the gods in all things.

After this, she wedded Cupid, who never flew away from her again. Apollo sang, and Venus, her anger forgotten, danced at the wedding.

Juno and Halcyone

From her golden throne on Mount Olympus, the goddess Juno could look down and see all that happened on the earth. She watched over the fortunes of good women among the mortals, and was the special protectress of brides. Her two special birds—the peacock and the cuckoo—might often be seen near her. On the steps of her throne slept her messenger, Iris, always half-awake, and ready to dart down like a bird, to the earth, to the underworld, or to any other place where Juno might send her.

Iris was the granddaughter of Old Ocean. Her sisters were the Dark Clouds; her bridge was the rainbow, which joined heaven to earth. She had golden wings, and her draperies were as many-colored as her bridge, which was made of the most beautiful flower-tints ever seen.

One of Juno's most faithful worshippers was Halcyone, the wife of King Ceyx of Thessaly. It happened that King Ceyx was obliged to take a distant journey, far away over the seas. One night during his absence a very heavy storm came up, and the winds blew a gale.

Halcyone, being the daughter of the wind-god, Aeolus, knew well what her brothers, the Winds, could do, and passed the night in great terror. The next day she walked back and forth all day on the shore, longing for tidings of her husband's ship, yet fearing to know what might have happened. She was almost beside herself with worry, and did not know what to do. At last, toward night, she carried wreaths to Juno's temple, and implored help from the goddess.

Juno knew all that had happened during the storm—how the king's ship had been broken to pieces upon the rocks, and how poor King Ceyx was already floating with the seaweed.

But the gods could do wonderful things. At a word from Juno, Iris set her beautiful rainbow bridge in the sky, while her sisters, the Dark Clouds, gathered together behind it. She came swiftly down the bridge to the earth, then flew toward the cave of Somnus, the god of sleep and dreams. She flew low over great fields of scarlet poppies—the poppies that bring sleep—and heard the trickling water of the river Lethe, which had its source within the cave of Somnus. Soon she reached the dark, cool, silent cave, and there lay Somnus, sleeping very soundly, on a great bed heaped high with black feathers. Around the god were dreams of every kind— good dreams and bad dreams, beautiful dreams and ugly dreams, true dreams and false dreams. As Iris entered, her coming lit up the darkness, and the wonderful colors of her garments shone to the farthest recess of the cave. She roused Somnus and delivered Juno's message.

That night Somnus sent a dream to Halcyone—a dream of a wreck at a place some distance down the coast. Early the next morning, Halcyone ran to the place of which she had dreamed. Some distance from

The next day she walked back and forth all day on the shore.

the shore, she saw floating beams, and something bright among them—something which shone like the king's crown. Feeling a sudden longing to go to this spot, she started forward, and immediately felt herself raised on wings and carried out over the tossing waves; for Juno had changed her into a bird with plumage of Iris's own colors. With a loud cry, Halcyone flew to her Ceyx. Just as she lit on the floating beams, the bright crown became a crest of feathers, and the dead king a living bird with plumage like Halcyone's own.

So Ceyx and Halcyone were not separated after all. They lived happily as a pair of kingfishers in the fresh air and bright sunshine. Every year thereafter, the two birds built a nest which floated on the sea. During the fourteen days that Halcyone sat hatching her brood, nary a breath of wind stirred, and the sea stayed smooth as glass under Aeolus's careful watch. From that time on, days of fine weather and calm seas, in midwinter, have been called "halcyon days."

Atalanta and the Footrace

When Atalanta was born, her father, the King of Arcadia, was angered. He wanted sturdy sons who would fight for him, not a daughter. Bitterly disappointed, he ordered that the baby princess be left to perish on the Parthenian Hill. A she-bear, hearing the child's piteous cries, carried it off to her lair, where she suckled it with her young and raised it as one of her own cubs. Atalanta grew as strong as any other wild creature of the forest.

Years later, when hunters came to the lair to kill the bear, they were amazed to find a fearless white-skinned woman who fought for her life and bit them as savagely as her foster brothers did. Under the care of the hunters, Atalanta grew into a maiden whose beauty was matched by her strength and courage. She ran as swift as the wind, and the shafts that her strong arm sped from her bow struck straight to the heart of any beast that she chased.

At length, when her father learned that the beautiful huntress whom people spoke of as only second to the goddess Diana in her skill at hunting was his daughter, he accepted her as his child. Her father hoped to marry her to one of the great heroes of their land, but Atalanta would settle for no one whom she thought was not a good match for her.

"If any man wants to be my husband," Atalanta told her father, "then he must be ready to face for my sake even the loss of dear life itself. I shall be the prize of him who outruns me in a footrace. But he who tries and fails must pay to Death his penalty."

One after another, suitors came to race the maiden whose face bewitched them and whose strength they admired, but no mortal man was as fleet as Atalanta.

Each day, a youth would challenge to race her for her hand, and each day, as the race ended, another youth paid the price of his defeat.

Among those who longed for Atalanta's hand was Milanion, a beautiful youth who pled his case to the goddess. In sympathy, Aphrodite gave Milanion three golden apples that grew on a tree in the garden of her temple, and she told him how he might use them to claim Atalanta as his bride. The next day, Milanion challenged Atalanta to a race.

"Thou art tempted by the deathless gods," said she. "I pity you Milanion, for when you race with me this day, it shall be your last."

And so the race began. Scarcely did the feet of either seem to touch the ground, all who watched agreed that this was a race worthy for the gods to behold.

But as they ran, almost abreast so that none could tell which was the gainer, Milanion obeyed the bidding of Aphrodite and let fall one of the golden apples. Never before had Atalanta beheld an apple of solid gold. She stopped to pick up the treasure.

She stopped to pick up the treasure.

Milanion had sped several paces ahead, and as Atalanta came abreast of him again, he dropped the second apple. Again, Atalanta gave in to temptation to pick it up, as Milanion sped ahead of her. Again, Atlanta gained the ground that she lost, and again Milanion dropped an apple of gold for Atalanta to stoop and retrieve.

A mighty shout arose from those standing at the finish line as Milanion finished a half step ahead of Atalanta. Not only had Milanion won the race, he had won the hand of the beautiful huntress whose heart, as cold and remote as the snow on Mount Olympus, he knew that he could warm.

Jason and the Golden Fleece

J ason was the son of King Aeson, and heir to his father's kingdom of Iolcus. One day, when Jason was a young boy, a warrior chief named Pelias came to the palace with a great body of armed men, and broke through the gates. King Aeson fled with his young son across the swamps to a cave that he knew was home to Chiron.

Kneeling by his son Aeson pointed into the cave and said, "Fear not, but go in, and whomsoever you shall find, lay your hands upon his knees, and say, 'In the name of Zeus, the father of gods and men, I am your guest from this day forth.'"

Fear not, but go in.

Now Chiron was a centaur. Like all centaurs, he had the body and legs of a horse, and the head and shoulders of a man. He supported himself by keeping a kind of school, and his pupils became very expert horsemen and soldiers skilled in the use of spear and shield. Chiron's school was a rough, wild one, but it made brave men, as it did of Jason.

Meanwhile, Pelias reigned in Iolcus, but his reign was not free of trouble. For a prophecy had been made that Pelias should beware of a man who would one day come down from the mountains, wearing only one sandal.

When Jason was twenty years old, he was a strong, handsome youth. Being old enough to try his strength, he bade good-bye to Chiron, threw a leopard's skin over his shoulders, and taking a spear in each hand, set out for Iolcus, intending to take it back from Pelias.

On his way down the mountain, Jason came to a stream which was badly swollen, and on the bank he saw an old woman who did not dare to cross. He kindly offered to carry her over, and his offer was accepted. He noticed that she looked very small and thin, and thought she would be very light to carry, but when he had fairly entered the stream, he found her very heavy. In his effort to fight against the current, and at the same time to stand up under his burden, he left one of his sandals sticking in the mud at the bottom of the river. But he succeeded in reaching the opposite shore, where he set the little old woman down in safety. Imagine his astonishment to find that he had carried the great goddess, Juno, across the stream. From this time forward, Juno was Jason's friend.

When Jason walked into the forum at Iolcus, the people thought a god had come, and wondered whether the stranger was not Apollo or Mars. But King Pelias, remembering the prophecy, gave a quick glance at Jason's feet, and saw only one sandal. With much misgiving he asked the stranger's name.

Jason told Pelias who he was, and how he had been brought up in Chiron's cave. The news spread quickly through the town, and after Jason's kinsmen, the sons of Aeolus, heard it, they welcomed him to their houses.

After Jason had been in Iolcus for about five days, he gathered his kinsmen together, and went before Pelias

JASON CAME TO A STREAM WHICH WAS BADLY SWOLLEN, AND ON THE BANK
HE SAW AN OLD WOMAN WHO DID NOT DARE TO CROSS.

and the people to present his claim to the throne. Since he and Pelias were kinsmen, he did not think it right that there should be fighting and bloodshed between them. So he consented to give up to Pelias much of the land and many of the flocks and herds which were his by right, but said that he must have the throne and scepter.

Pelias showed no anger at this demand of Jason's, but he quickly devised a plan for sending the hero away again. He said that a few nights before Jason's arrival he had had a very strange dream. In this dream a voice had commanded him to go to Colchis, and bring back the Golden Fleece of the ram which had carried Phrixus across the sea to Colchis.

The story of Phrixus was well known to Jason and to all the people of Iolcus. Many years before this, two children of the race of Aeolus—Phrixus and Helle—who were persecuted by their stepmother, fled away from Iolcus with the help of a ram with golden fleece. The ram had taken the two children on its back, and had swum across the sea to the kingdom of Colchis. On the way, at a place where the water was very rough, Helle had fallen off and been swept away; but Phrixus had clung tightly to the ram's fleece, and arrived safe at Colchis. There, the ram was sacrificed to Jupiter. Phrixus gave its beautiful golden fleece to the king of Colchis, who nailed it on a great oak tree, in the Garden of Mars. All these things had happened so very, very long before this, that the people of Iolcus had now almost forgotten that Phrixus and Helle had ever lived; but they remembered what their fathers had told them about the wonderful Golden Fleece, and many of them thought that the fleece should be brought back to Iolcus.

After telling his dream, King Pelias went on to say: "I should like nothing better than to obey the voice I heard in my dream; but I am far too old for such an enterprise. You, Jason, are young and strong. You had better go in my place. If you succeed in this, and thereby prove yourself able to rule over the people of Iolcus, you shall have your father's crown and throne."

The chiefs who attended Pelias all thought this fair. They said that a young man's courage should be proved, and that if Jason were really fit for the throne, he would bring back the fleece. Jason's uncles and cousins said that if he attempted this task, he should not go alone, for he would encounter grave dangers along the way.

A call went out in the marketplace for volunteers to accompany Jason, and it was answered by the bravest young men from all parts of Greece. Jason then asked the master shipbuilder, Argus, to build him a galley of sixty oars, the biggest ship ever built. In honor of Argus's hard work, the ship was christened the Argo.

In those days anyone who sailed far out into the open sea was likely to encounter all sorts of strange monsters and unknown terrors. The Argonauts, as these heroes came to be known, had not sailed many miles before they saw a number of Harpies hovering over a rocky cape that jutted out into the sea. The Harpies were great birds, like giant vultures, with the faces of women.

As the Argonauts came nearer the cape, they could see that these horrible Harpies were tormenting a blind old man who sat among the trees in his garden, trying to eat his breakfast. Just as he had raised a morsel of food to his mouth, a Harpy would swoop down with a great rush of wings and snatch it away. Feeling sorry for the poor old king, Jason's crew drove the Harpies away.

The king, whose name was Phineus, was very grateful, and when he heard that the Argonauts were voyaging to Colchis, he told them a safe way through the Symplegades, two huge rocks which they would have to pass between when they entered the Black Sea.

Many a good ship had been crushed by the Symplegades; for when any moving object passed between them, they had a trick of whirling around on their bases, and crashing together with a force that would grind almost any substance into powder. To avoid such a calamity, King Phineus advised the Argonauts to send a dove through the narrow passage between the rocks first, and then the moment that the rocks began to swing open again to row the Argo through with all possible speed.

The next day, when the Argo reached the Symplegades, Jason followed the advice of King Phineus, and sent the swiftest of his doves between them. The huge rocks smashed together with a roar like thunder, then began to move slowly back to their places. Quickly, the Argo shot through. The rocks crashed together with such force that they could not separate themselves. Thus, the Sympleglades never crushed another ship.

The Argonauts sailed a long way farther, and saw many strange things. One day, they passed the Island of Mars, where the Stymphalian birds built their nests, and here they found two sons of Phrixus who had been shipwrecked. They took these men into their ship, and gave them food and clothing. From them they found out that Aetes, the king of Colchis, was a cruel and wicked man whom they would have good reason to fear; and, worse, that the Golden Fleece was guarded by a most frightful dragon.

The next day, after anchoring the Argo in a secret harbor, Jason went straight to King Aetes, and told him on what errand he had come.

"Oho! So you wish to take the Golden Fleece home with you?" said Aetes. "Well, you are welcome to take it, but only if you will do me a favor, first. Yoke my bulls, there, to the plow, and plow a few acres in the Field of Mars, then sow it with these dragon's teeth. These teeth are from the same dragon that Cadmus killed. Mars gave them to me as a present."

Medea, the king's daughter, stood by his side when Jason presented himself, and her dark eyes lit up at the sight of the hero's beauty. She was the niece of Circe, the famous enchantress, and she had learned from her aunt the use of many medicinal and poisonous herbs. She knew certain charms and enchantments, too, and had secret rooms in her father's palace where a kettle full of a mysterious mixture was always boiling. While her father entertained the Argonauts, Medea found Jason alone and gave him a powerful ointment made in her kettle. She also gave him a little violet flower, which had been brought from the banks of the river Lethe.

The day after Jason had received these gifts from Medea, King Aetes proposed to entertain his guests with games held in the Field of Mars. After a few races had been run, the king said that Jason should now plow an acre with the bulls, and then sow the dragon's teeth. After that, he was welcome to take the Golden Fleece from the tree where it hung, and carry it home to Iolcus.

Aetes's bulls were magnificent creatures. Their white horns were tipped with sharp steel points, and their hooves of solid brass struck sparks from the paving stones when they were led from their stable. As Jason approached them, they lifted their heads and snorted, sending a shower of gleaming sparks flying from their nostrils. As they pawed up the earth with their brass hooves, the grass all around them took fire.

No one but Jason and Medea knew that, that morning, Jason had covered himself from head to foot with the protective ointment that Medea had given him. So Jason walked fearlessly up to the bulls and put the yoke on their necks, amazing the crowd with his courageousness.

After plowing his acre, Jason sowed the dragon's teeth in the furrows, then covered them over with soil. He had heard the story of Cadmus, and the dragon's teeth that could raise an army of fierce warriors, and only half believed it. But the teeth began to sprout and grow, just as they had for Cadmus. First, a few steel spearheads thrust up through the ground; then the soil all over the ploughed acre began to heave, and before Jason knew what had happened, there stood rows of warriors, all armed, and looking very fierce. Seeing Jason, the warriors all raised their spears with a great cry, and would have attacked him. But Jason snatched off his helmet and hurled it into the throng, striking several of the soldiers. Then each warrior thought that he had been attacked by his brothers. So they all began to fight among themselves, and continued fighting till every one was slain. When the last armed warrior of the dragon's brood had fallen, the Argonauts sent up a loud cheer for their leader, and brought wreaths and crowned him, as they were accustomed to do when a hero won in the games.

King Aetes could not now deny to Jason the right to take the Golden Fleece. With great reluctance, he showed Jason the way to the Grove of Mars, where the Golden Fleece hung.

The Grove of Mars stood in a valley, called the Garden of Mars, which could be entered only through a narrow ravine between two high rocks. A rapid stream ran between the rocks, and sometimes the dragon lay in this stream, guarding the way. Sometimes, too, the

Her dark eyes lit up at the sight of the hero's beauty.

But Jason snatched off his helmet and hurled it into the throng,
striking several of the soldiers.

dragon used to coil itself around the oak where the fleece hung. It was always somewhere in the valley, and was sure to be wakeful and watching.

The Garden of Mars was certainly not a beautiful garden. Everything in it seemed to have been struck by a blight. The earth produced no grass, but was covered instead by bare, brown rocks whose edges looked sharp and dangerous. The trees bore thorns instead of leaves, and their branches were twisted into sinister shapes.

Indeed, the Golden Fleece was the one bright spot in the whole garden. It hung on a low branch of the giant oak, and seemed to throw off flakes of light. And there, coiled around the huge trunk of the oak, was the dragon. It was spotted and blotched, and had a sharp-pointed, fierce-looking crest. It looked very ugly and dangerous.

As Jason came nearer to the oak, the dragon raised its crest and began to roar and bellow so loud that the sound could be heard all the way to Colchis. But Jason carried in his hand the little violet flower which Medea had plucked on the banks of Lethe. He held this flower out before him, at arm's length, and the moment the dragon smelt its strange odor, it lowered its drooping head, closed its fierce eyes, and fell into a deep sleep.

Then Jason took down the beautiful Golden Fleece from the oak, and went to tell his Argonauts that he had conquered the dragon. They all agreed that they had better sail for home while it was still night. And while the heroes were getting the Argo under way, Medea stole away from the palace and joined them.

By the time the sun rose, the next morning, they were well out to sea. Word was brought to King Aetes that the Argonauts had taken the Golden Fleece and gone, and that Medea had gone with them. The king went down to the shore with a great company of armed men, and sent some of his war galleys after the Argo; but the Argo left the Colchian ships far behind, and soon passed out of sight.

The heroes reached Iolcus safely, and Pelias honored his promise to give Jason the throne and the scepter. And Jason reigned long and happily in the place of King Pelias, the usurper.

THE MOMENT THE DRAGON SMELT ITS STRANGE ODOR, IT LOWERED ITS
DROOPING HEAD, CLOSED ITS FIERCE EYES, AND FELL INTO A DEEP SLEEP.